The Insect Makers.

By Peter Plant
Illustrated By Phil Worth

All rights reserved, no part of this publication may be reproduced by any means, electronic, mechanical photocopying, documentary, film or in any other format without prior written permission of the publisher.

> Published by
> Chipmunkapublishing
> United Kingdom

http://www.chipmunkapublishing.com

Copyright © 2017 Peter Plant
ISBN   978-1-78382-325-3

The insect makers.

'for my beautiful grandchildren Ruby ,Lily, Rosie and Archie'

Peter Plant

The insect makers.

Nearly 12 thousand years ago, after a terrible ice-age that only the snowmen enjoyed, our world was in a sorry state. Even the remaining trees, despite wearing scarves and gloves had given up the hope of ever feeling the warmth of our earth again. They had lost the will to grow strong and produce leaves.

But over time, as the snow and ice had begun to thaw and the world gradually warmed the first makers appeared. There were only four of them on that visit: the tree maker, the fern maker, the bluebell maker and the grass maker. They felt sad to see our

World suffering but happy in the fact that they could begin to put things right. They roamed the world planting bulbs and seeds and when their job was done they disappeared.

The work that the early makers had carried out long ago was a complete success; the trees had grown tall and strong and in the forests lush green ferns had carpeted the floor along with the gorgeous bluebells. The grassland in-between the forests was so fresh, vivid green and unspoilt that it would have taken your breath away.

Then, one day, when the sun was high and bright, our world was about to change. Not a sound could be heard. The rustling of the forest leaves fell silent. It was as if the trees knew the moment long awaited for had finally arrived. The silence was only broken by the bluebells softly tinkling their bells.

The insect makers.

One by one, appearing through the proud trees and ferns onto an area of grassland the makers appeared. They were breathtaking. Tall, Ablaze in gold, long golden hair and beards reaching down to their waists, Golden skin, but most striking of all were their large golden eyes. Instead of a pupil, in the centre of these eyes were tiny images of all the living things they were about to make. The bird maker had a tiny robin in each eye, the fish-maker a goldfish, the flower maker a stunning red rose. Then there was the frog and toad maker, he had a frog in one eye and a toad in the other. So many makers! There was the deer maker, the unicorn maker, the badger maker, the mouse maker, the rabbit and hare maker, there were makers everywhere! They wore long green cloaks touching the floor and on the backs of their cloaks, beautifully embroidered in fine golden thread were the same, but much larger images than in their eyes of the tasks they had been chosen to do. When they smiled the world trembled slightly in excitement. They carried boxes, and in each box were all the ingredients needed to form the living breathing life that we see around us today.

Only one person knew where the makers came from. Future generations say that the first makers had magical bulbs that they planted and they grew slowly among the bluebells and ferns underneath the tall trees that were developing. Others that they were formed in hidden caves in the forests that were lined with gold. Many believed that they slid down rainbows onto the fresh world.

Before going their separate ways the makers formed small circles and sat on their boxes talking and singing songs to which all the tiny creatures in their eyes danced along to. They all laughed at the frog and toad maker whose eyes leapt up and down making him look as though he was winking at everyone! All of them were incredibly excited by the tasks ahead. All but one- the insect maker- of course he was delighted to be selected to become a maker but he couldn't share in the festivities as wholeheartedly as the others. He felt his job would be never ending. It's not really fair, he thought. There are so many insects and creepy crawlies to be made, thousands more than his friends had to make. But on the plus side though, if there could be a plus side, the makers with incredibly hard tasks had been granted permission to form just one of the species they had been chosen to create. Those like the insect maker, the bird maker, the fish maker and so on. They would form just one and when the sun set and darkness descended onto the new world the night makers began their work. They would silently visit the new creations and gently stroke them while they slept and as the sun rose again there would be several more beautiful creatures.

Of course the makers with relatively simpler jobs such as forming the badger, fox, hedgehog didn't need to rely on the night makers. They had been instructed to only make several moms and dads of each newly created amazing animals.

The sun was losing itself behind the trees. The makers stood and shook each other's hands and wished one another the best of luck. After going their separate ways the insect maker found himself a grassy hollow at the base of a hill. He settled down to sleep. As he lay on the sweet green grass he whispered to himself 'please send me a helper'.

The insect makers.

When the master awoke the peep-red sun was just showing himself above the trees. It was still a little misty and the redness of the sun bathed the landscape with hues of orange and red that humbled all who looked at the beauty of the stunning scene. The hoverflies in his eyes fluttered their wings to help him wake fully after a disturbed sleep. When they settled down and tucked their tiny wings back by their sides the master saw a figure looking down on him. It was a little girl. 'Good morning master, someone has sent me to help you, when shall we start because I'm very excited'. The master knew who had sent her to help him and was beside himself with joy. He approached the girl, bent down on one knee and held her hand. 'What's your name little one?' 'Ruby' she replied. 'That's a lovely name Ruby'. She didn't have the same appearance as the master makers, she was just a pretty little girl. In fact poor Ruby didn't have a clue where she came from. She was hoping that she was in a wonderful dream that she wouldn't wake up from. Ruby had long brown hair and hazel eyes and a quaint little nose like a button mushroom, and she was blessed with a smile that would melt the hearts of the makers she would encounter on her journey. Ruby's cloak was green though. Decorated on the back with the same golden thread that the makers had embroidered on their cloaks. The image was of little boys and girls in the long lush grass playing and laughing under a bright yellow sun. Ruby also had a box, a little smaller than the master's but full of all the items needed to create the insects that the insect maker would think were suitable for Ruby to make.

The master maker quickly put together a list of the insects he thought Ruby could tackle. He wanted to protect her from the more nasty creepy crawlies. Things like fleas and flies, wasps, spiders, earwigs, mosquitos, horrible mantises all things with stings except for the bumble bee. Bog eyed beetles bug eyed beetles dung beetles- Ruby didn't need to know that some beetles spent their entire life rolling balls of poo around and falling out as to who had the biggest ball!
When the master had carefully drawn up a list of the insects he

thought were suitable for Ruby to make. He sat her down and after a glass of warm milk that he had scrounged from the cow maker he explained that there were no pictures to work from, she had to use her own imagination. 'One important thing though Ruby' the master explained 'before you set them away into the new world you must whisper them some words of encouragement or any dangers they might need to avoid'.

Ruby was mega-excited. Who shall I start with she thought? She looked down the list and came across the ladybird. 'What a lovely name' she whispered to herself. Yes ladybird! She will be my first. Ruby opened up her magic box. The contents were amazing. It had small compartments which contained all the little body parts needed to make an insect. One section contained legs of all shapes and sizes: little legs hairy legs long legs fat legs thin legs leg's bent in all directions, legs beautifully coloured, every type of leg imaginable to create these fabulous little creatures. The wing section was just as weird and wonderful: shell like, long and transparent with veins showing short and transparent with veins showing, black wings green wings beautiful wings full of colour, striped wings, all waiting to fly off into the new world. There was an eye compartment: bug eyes big eyes little eyes that were to be glued together to make one big eye- that's weird thought Ruby- eyes on sticks, the list was endless. In another compartment were furry colourful strips of thin material that could be cut and shaped with tiny scissors that would make up any insect that required furry little body parts. Stings-won't be using them thought Ruby. Strange looking long things for the front of their heads-antennae- the master called them. In the box were small pots of paint and tiny brushes that Ruby could use if she wanted to change the colour of any body part.

But the most important ingredient in the box- buggloop! This was a sort of putty, softer and easier to shape than things like playdough or blue-tack. It could be shaped easily into any form of body part. Buggloop came with little sticks that she could use for creating patterns onto the insects.

Right thought Ruby, let's get started. Ruby took out a little felt lined tray that she could work on. This would prevent any damage to the insects in case she dropped one of them. She excitedly took a pinch of buggloop and moulded it into a little ball. Then added tiny legs and a small head with little antennae facing forwards. Now, what type of wings, she rummaged through the wing compartment and decided on the shape she thought most fitting for the ladybird. She carefully took them out using tiny tweezers and placed them into the tray. Then she gently eased the front of the wings into the buggloop. Perfect she thought. Mmm don't like the colour though. The wings were perfectly shaped to suit Ruby's vision of what the ladybird should look like but they were a dull grey. That won't do thought Ruby. She searched through the

tiny pots of paint and decided on
a colour scheme of red and black.
She took out the paint and 2 little
brushes then coated the wings
with a lovely bright shiny red.
Ruby's brain was ticking over.
Yes I know, she carefully dipped
the other brush into the black
paint and began to add spots-one
two three four five six seven- yes
that's enough-the ladybird was
finished. Makers didn't need
fairy dust or magical particles to
bring their creations to life; they
just breathed on them. Not
blowing through pursed lips
which would have blown them
sky high, but opening their
mouths and breathing softly on
them. Ruby was granted
permission by the master to be

able to use this mysterious power for the time she was helping him and was so excited that she breathed onto the ladybird too soon and she stirred into life. The ladybird was ready to fly off, but to Ruby's horror she had forgotten the masters instructions- 'before you send them on their way you must offer some words of encouragement or any possible dangers they may encounter'. 'Don't fly off yet little ladybird' Ruby whispered. The ladybird settled down.

'Seven spots I've given you, one for every day
And shiny wings to help you on your way.

In the shimmering sun you'll have your fun
But be careful little one
There'll be creatures out there, without a care
Whose beaks would see you gone'.

'Away, off you go my lovely lady' Ruby proudly bubbled. The ladybird turned to face Ruby. She felt sure she was thanking her, then she turned round and flew into the fresh new world. The ladybird circled around and landed on the back of the master maker's hand. 'Yes she's made a wonderful job of you hasn't she'. The ladybird fluttered her wings and was gone. Ruby was so happy and excited she jumped for joy, caught her leg on the magical box, tripped over and lay giggling in the warm sumptuous grass. The master was delighted for her.

After the excitement of making her first insect and the early morning start ruby closed her eyes and fell into a dreamy sleep. She dreamt of being cradled in the arms of a tender beautiful lady in a strange setting. The lady then placed her gently into a crib made of bluebells, poppies and soft ferns, kissed her and whispered 'sleep now little Ruby your time will soon come'. Ruby woke to the sensation of something tickling her feet. She looked down and saw 2 robins perched on her big toes. The little birds then fluttered around Ruby's head several times and flew off into the bright sky. She sensed that they were enticing her to rise and continue the good work she had begun.

When Ruby stood she was astonished by everything around her. As well as the robins other colourful birds were gliding and twittering in the sky and cows, sheep, colourful deer were all grazing peacefully. Rabbits and hares were bobbing and dancing in the bright sunshine.

Right, who next, thought Ruby excitedly looking down her list of projects. Bumble bee! I love that name. She thought hard using her imagination. 'Yes- Got it'! Ruby shouted excitedly, she began by moulding 2 segments of the bee using her buggloop then searched through the furry little coats until she settled on a colour scheme. Yellow collar, brown middle section then the rear end of brown with a white bum. She carefully cut the furry coats with her tiny scissors and wrapped them round the buggloop gently squeezing them into position. The buggloop, as well as having special qualities that enabled Ruby to squish and swash it into any shape or form also had sticky qualities that made it possible for the furry strips to stick perfectly onto the buggloop. 6 little hairy legs were inserted then Ruby began searching for the type of wings that would best suit the little bumbly bee. The master maker had become so curious watching Ruby snip and stick and work feverously on her new creation that he walked over to her. 'Ah, the bumble bee' enquired the master. 'He is such an important member of our family'. He explained his ideas of the role the little bee was to play in helping spread flowers and colour to the new world. 'Pick the legs carefully Ruby' said the master. 'This little beauty will collect something called pollen from the flowers it will settle on, then spread the pollen from his legs to other flowers making more flowers'. Ruby was a bit baffled but sort of understood. She swapped the legs for ones that were more sturdy and hairy. Lovely veined wings were inserted into the buggloop. 'I'm afraid you'll have to give the lad a sting Ruby'. Ruby was horrified! 'But he's so lovely I don't want him to sting anything'. 'Don't worry Ruby' said the master 'he won't sting anything unless they try to damage the nest with the queen inside. They're not horrible and nasty like the wasp I'm about to make'. Ruby reluctantly shoved a sting into the bee's bum. 'Don't forget to wish him well' he said before returning to his place of work. Ruby looked at her latest lovely creation and before breathing on him offered up a few words:

'Fat and furry but not as scary as the drunken stingy wasp.
In the hearts of flowers you'll spend your hours
Collecting pollen in your sacs.
Then spread the flowers in the summery hours
From your knees you bumbly bees.
Ruby breathed on the beautiful bee and off he flew making a lovely buzzing sound.

Ruby was buzzing as well, she was so proud of herself for making her first 2 little friends she sat on her box and thought how wonderful it would be to meet and watch other makers at work. She asked permission from the master if she could explore the surrounding countryside. 'Yes of course Ruby, I'll come with you in case you get lost'. The master and Ruby climbed the gently sloping grassy bank behind them. When they reached the top Ruby gasped in amazement at the view that struck her. Below them was a beautiful valley with sloping hills. At the bottom was a stream that fed pools of water on either side. The pools were deep blue and with the reflection of the butter yellow sun it gave Ruby the impression of proud eyes overseeing the birth of a new and wonderful world. Occasionally fluffy white clouds passed over the sun casting moving shadows across the landscape. She looked up at the sky and sure enough sitting on one of the clouds a maker was hard at work. He held a pole with a large circular ring attached, very similar to what the incoming children will use when they form bubbles by dipping it into a little container. He dipped his circular ring into the cloud he was sitting on and gently blew lovely fluffy clouds into the sky. Awesome, thought Ruby.

The insect makers.

Looking down into the valley Ruby could just make out the figure of a maker at the edge of one of the pools. The fish-maker she thought. She looked all around and saw other makers at work. 'Could we meet some of them?' asked Ruby. 'Yes of course' he replied. Hand in hand they descended into the valley. The first maker they came across was the unicorn maker. There was something wrong, thought

Ruby. The horn had disappeared from his eyes and the back of his beautifully embroidered cloak. 'What's happened?' inquired the insect maker. The unicorn maker was a little dejected but couldn't help but smile when he saw Ruby. 'This is my helper Ruby' explained the master. The unicorn maker was delighted to meet Ruby. 'Well I've had some bad luck with my unicorns. Every-time they tried to graze on the scrumptious grass they kept getting their horns stuck in rabbit holes, mole holes, badger holes and any other hole that the maker of furry things that live underground has made for his family. Of course it's not his fault, lots of lovely furry creatures were selected to live underground. But sadly I've had to discard the horn and now I'm officially the horse maker'. 'O dear' sympathised Ruby 'the horses are lovely though master'. 'Yes they are Ruby' replied the now horse maker. 'But don't fret Ruby I will make sure that all the children who will appear soon will see the unicorn in their dreams and the unicorn will live on in folklore'.

Ruby and the master wished the horse maker well and continued into the valley. The first pool they came across was tended by the fish-maker. Once again Ruby was awestruck by the beauty of the pool. Large lily pads grew in the shallow margins, in between the pads striking yellow flowers had opened with the warmth of the sun. The pool was surrounded by reeds that gently rustled in the slight summer breeze.

The insect makers.

After introducing Ruby the insect maker inquired as to the success he was having making fish. The fish-maker was wet through; every time he released a fish into the water the fish flapped its tail and soaked him to the skin. He was more than happy though because it cooled him down on such a hot day. 'Well I had a few teething problems' explained the fish-maker. 'I thought I'd start with the little stickleback. I gave him some small spikes on his back but was unsure how much fishgloop I should use. 'I tied a tiny length of golden thread to his tail in case I hadn't used enough and sure enough he took to the skies-not enough fishgloop- he did a few loop-de-loops before hurtling towards me landing spikes first on my forehead! I managed to eventually prise my little friend from my head, added a little more fishgloop and away he went. Got any plasters'? 'I had a few problems with my goldfish as well-too much fishgloop! He sank like a stone. I had to wade in and gently remove some fishgloop from his fat tummy. He was ticklish and thrashed about in bouts of laughter. When I got it right he leapt out the water gave me a fishy kiss before swimming off blissfully happy.

 'I've decided to save the pike till last'. Ruby saw a tear well in the fishmakers eye. 'What's a pike master'? enquired Ruby. 'Well it might upset you little Ruby but the pike will eat some of the fish'. Ruby was mortified. 'Why'? She inquired. 'It's called the balance of nature Ruby. If we didn't create these nasty creatures the pool would become too overcrowded with fish and there wouldn't be enough food to go round and they would become very hungry. I know it's sad Ruby but don't you worry I'm going to talk to him very sternly. This is what I'm going to say:

I had no choice but to create your toothy grin
Because after all you've committed no great sin
But if you don't pick on the old and ill
I'll dive in and punch you under the chin.

 The flower maker was hard at work. 'How's it going flower maker'? Enquired the insect maker. 'It was going great till a little while ago. Here I am in peaceful harmony with my flowers and suddenly I was disturbed by a little creature with a coloured coat buzzing around my head, landing on the flowers and completely distracting me. He's gone now though, I'm sure he meant no harm it was just the buzzing that was making it hard to concentrate'. Ruby blushed a little, she knew the culprit, it was her lovely little bumble bee.

On another beautiful blue pool they came across the frog and toad maker. He shook the insect makers hand and bent down to greet Ruby. She smiled at the frog and toad maker and his heart skipped a beat. 'Lovely to meet you Ruby, I hope you're making spectacular little insects for your master'. 'Yes she is, Ruby is being a great help to me'. Ruby was fascinated as to how the frog and toad maker went about his work. 'Well the frogs were fairly easy Ruby' explained the master, 'lots of froggloop especially to their strong back legs, big eyes, and I painted them green. Before I set them on their way I gave them some encouraging words, would you like to know what I said to them Ruby'? 'Yes please master'. The master frog and toad maker recited his words of wisdom:

Hipperty hop my little friends
find a pool to lay your spawn
Where your tadpoles will dance into an early springtime dawn.
But hide them away as best you can in the weeds and the reeds

Where they'll feed. Because the children will come in the midday sun
To have fun, with nets that will reach so far
and some of your squiggly tadpoles could well end up in a jar!

'When I breathed on them away they hopped on their strong back legs, wonderful swimmers too. They certainly didn't need arm bands or a rubber ring. They took to the water gracefully using a breast stroke action which was amazing to watch'.
'Unfortunately I made a bit of a mess with the toad. I breathed on him early to check that he could jump like the frogs but didn't use

enough toadgloop on his back legs which meant he could only crawl and then to top it all I spilt brown paint all over him making him a little drab looking. I picked him up to try to make adjustments but didn't realise that I still had some tiny little blobs of toadgloop sticking to my fingers. I had to explain the awful situation we were in and that I intended to put things right. To mine and his horror I had transferred some of these little blobs onto his back making him look as though he was covered in warts. He looked at me in disgust, stuck his tongue out and crawled into the damp grass at the water's edge, I tried to find him to apologise and to improve his looks but he was hiding somewhere thinking I don't want that maker to come anywhere near me again. The worst thing of it all though was that I had to make mommy toad exactly the same! She wasn't best pleased either, in fact she stuck her tongue out as well before crawling away to find her partner in the wet grass'.

By the time the master and Ruby had met several more makers the sun was beginning to set. He suggested that should make their way back to their working area, pack away their boxes and settle down to sleep. She lay on the grass and wrapped her cloak around herself. As she lay there she couldn't help but thank the stars for being so lucky. She thought about her ladybird and bumbly bee and prayed that they would be safe and live a peaceful and happy life. What would lay in store for her tomorrow she thought before nodding off to sleep.

In the morning after having a breakfast of milk and cornflakes- made by the cornflake maker- Ruby checked her list again. Who's next she thought. Dragonfly-that sounds like a challenge. Ruby closed her eyes and imagined what a dragon fly should look like. Dragon sounds scary. Ruby had heard tales that there were real dragon makers far away. Their dragons were huge and breathed fire. She asked the master if it was true. 'Yes it is I'm afraid Ruby, but don't worry the dragon makers arrived long before us and quickly realised that instead of making friendly dragons which was their intention they used far too much firegloop and the dragons gradually grew to enormous sizes, learned to breathe fire and began throwing their weight around. Although the makers all had their hair and beards singed by the fire they were fearless, all makers are fearless Ruby. They found ways round the problems though. They ordered them into deep dark caverns lined with gold. They knew dragons loved to protect riches and gold is certainly the richest material to protect. The makers then sealed the caverns making it impossible for them to ever terrorise the new world.

I'll make my dragonfly look just a little scary but completely harmless. Once again Ruby reached for her buggloop. I'll make him extra-long with big wings so other creatures will be a little wary of him. Ruby rolled out the buggloop thinner in the middle slightly thicker at the tail end and broader at the head this would enable Ruby to attach rather strange looking eyes. I'm going to make you colourful. Ruby painted the dragonfly black and then painted yellow bands all up its body and a little yellow triangle just behind the eyes. You'll be known as the Gold-Ringed Dragonfly. Little bent legs were attached to the thicker front end. Ruby sorted four fabulous long wings that you could see all the veins in. She studied her creation and thought; is he too scary? Will he frighten the children who would soon be arriving in the fresh new world? She could imagine the children sitting by a lovely pool having lunch and the dragonfly, appearing from nowhere, landing on the back of a little girl's hand! Oh we can't have that, I'll speak to him:

'Ablaze with fire you dragonfly
  Over pools and shallow streams

Don't go too close to the picnickers though
 They'll run away and scream!

The insect makers.

Ruby gently breathed on her latest creation and he took to the skies no doubt looking for a home by a lovely little pool.

Butterfly! How lovely is that name thought Ruby. She was now flying and becoming over confident. Then suddenly, like children often do, she felt a little naughty! Tee hee she thought to herself. She quickly formed the body parts and the legs. Right. The wings. Ruby selected four stunning looking white wings, added 4 black spots to help make the wings even more spectacular. Then the naughtiness crept in. What would happen if I added a tiny amount of buggloop to one of the wings. Let's see smiled Ruby. She carefully added some buggloop by spreading it to the underneath of just one wing and painted it white. Ruby spoke some words of wisdom even though she was now feeling a little guilty:

You'll be the prettiest insect in the air

Although we've yet to see you fly
Let's hope your lovely wings will flap
With gracefulness and flare. Be cautious
Though my little friend to avoid the spiders lair.

Ruby gently breathed on the butterfly and away it went. She clasped her hands to her mouth. O dear what have I done! The poor thing couldn't fly straight! She lurched about this way and that up and down forwards and backwards. Was she the ballerina of the sky? The master had been watching the poor butterfly struggling to fly straight. 'Ruby what have you done'? The master pretended to be stern. Ruby's bottom lip quivered trying hard not to cry. 'I'm sorry master I was just trying to experiment and it went wrong'. 'No more experimenting Ruby' 'Yes master' replied Ruby. Inside of course the master found the whole thing amusing. He thought to himself-O well I'm sure she will find her way in life and will eventually master the art of flying. In fact she flies in such a weird and wonderful way I'll give her a weird and wonderful name. She will be christened a cabbage white!

Ruby lay on the grass with a blade of grass between her lips and her hands behind her head feeling very proud of the work she had done so far. She knew the master was delighted for her even with the escapade of the poor butterfly.

Over the days Ruby had become entranced by the dense forests surrounding them, she'd never been in a forest before. She thought of a crafty plan to put to the master. She'd looked down her list and found a stick insect. She thought if I made one of these the master would allow her to take the little creature to the forest and place it on a branch of a tree and craftily spend a little time in the mysterious woods. Good idea sniggered Ruby. As good fortune would have it she may be able to go to the forest sooner than expected. The stick insect had to be very thin to resemble little twigs. Ruby tried to shape the buggloop into a twig but because it was so thin it kept drooping being unable to keep the thin shape. Ruby scratched her head trying to think of a way round the problem. Yes! She thought. If I could wrap a very thin layer of buggloop around a tiny twig that would maybe solve the problem. Ruby plucked up the courage to put the plan to the master. 'That sounds like a good idea Ruby, but don't stray too far into the forest because you may get lost'. When Ruby turned to go back to her workplace she could barely stifle a scream of joy. Of course the master knew of Ruby's plan to explore the forest and smiled to himself. He wasn't worried because he also knew the little forest people would bring her back safely.

Ruby gathered her little box together and headed for the woods. She tried to stop herself from running because she was so excited. She slowly entered the woods and placed her box next to a huge oak tree out of sight of the master. Ruby began walking further into the woods then stopped for a moment to fully take in the peace and tranquillity of the surrounding trees and lush ferns. Where the sun managed to break through the dense trees the ferns looked amazing, polka dotted with sunlight and with the green of the ferns made the whole scene really spectacular. She wasn't frightened at all, she sensed that in the quiet mystical beauty there was only goodness in the forest's heart. She ventured on before looking back and realising she was lost already. Ruby wasn't too worried because she knew the master would find her. Although she was a little worried that he may not be too pleased with her. She reached a breath-taking area where the bluebells completely covered the woodland floor. Ruby's mouth opened with the beauty of it all.

The insect makers.

In the distance, Ruby thought she saw a little girl standing waste deep among the bluebells. She rubbed her eyes to make sure she wasn't seeing things but the figure was still there. Ruby approached the girl with no fear in her heart. 'Hello Ruby, I knew you'd come to see us, I'm Lily the bluebell keeper'. Lily was astonishing to look at. Blue skinned and half as tall as Ruby with the most striking red hair and blue eyes imaginable. She wore a dress and hat that was exactly the shape and colour of a bluebell and in her beautiful hair there were ringlets of real bluebells. Ruby couldn't get her questions out quickly enough. 'What do you do Lily, how long have you been here, are there more of you'? 'I tend the bluebells Ruby, if any get damaged or lose their bells I repair them. My main job is yet to come though. When the first children walk in the forests they won't be able to contain their excitement and will skip and run through the bluebells. Of course they will mean no harm and in the dark nights I shall repair any damage done. I came with the first makers to help carry seeds and bulbs for them and asked permission to stay and tend the bluebells. They called me Lily the bluebell keeper and made this dress and hat for me'. 'But that was an age ago and you still look as young as me' said Ruby. 'Age is timeless here Ruby, others came after me when the trees had grown. I tend the bluebells until they go to sleep for the winter then I go to play with my friends Archie and Rosie the fern keepers'. Ruby looked round into the ferns and sure enough two figures waved at Ruby.

The insect makers.

They were completely green!
Their cloaks had large collars
reaching above their heads and
were cut and shaped to resemble

the ferns they tended. This is all so amazing thought Ruby. 'Did Archie and Rosie come with the first makers as well'? 'Yes we all carried baskets full of bulbs and seeds and they also asked for permission to stay, the makers were delighted that their work would be tended by such enthusiastic volunteers'.

'Come on Ruby, we'll show you around' enthused Rosie. Ruby, despite being barely 4 foot tall herself dwarfed the keepers but they held hands and led her further into the forest. They passed other makers hard at work. 'Hello Ruby' shouted the mushroom maker ',your cute little nose is very similar to the button mushrooms I'm creating'

Ruby laughed because she was naturally polite and replied 'yes it's perfect thank you, I can smell all the goodness of our new world'. The mushroom maker smiled and continued his work. Everywhere she looked new life was being born. She saw the fiery fox and the lovely badger digging his home. They all laughed watching the toadstool maker. Every time he created lovely colourful toadstools a wild boar followed the maker eating the toadstools he'd just planted! The toadstool maker eventually got very annoyed.' leave my toadstools alone, let them grow awhile .If you don't I'll speak to your master and ask him to remove your teeth'! The boar sulked off thinking I'll never eat anything without my teeth.

The insect makers.

Walking deeper into the woods Ruby was so overcome with emotion looking at the natural beauty surrounding her she sat down and began to cry. 'What troubles you Ruby, why do you cry'? Asked Lily sadly. 'It's not fair' said Ruby trying to stifle her tears 'everyone I've met seems to know why they are here and have beautiful garments and magical looks that tell the world of their purpose in being here. Apart from my lovely cloak and a nose that resembles a button mushroom'- at this point Ruby sobbed again. When she regained her composure Ruby continued. 'I just look out of place, and seemed to arrive as if in a dream. I just don't know where I came from'. 'Come with us', Lily held Ruby's hand and the four of them entered an avenue of trees almost like a cave formed of trees. In the distance a bright light shone and as Ruby approached the light she couldn't quite believe what she saw. Sitting in a large hollow of an ancient oak tree sat a glorious lady. She was surrounded by makers who had completed their tasks and dozens of keepers all sitting cross legged on the soft forest floor. Her striking beauty was even more breath-taking than the makers. She was bright silver with beautiful radiant hair topped by a halo like crown. The crown was interwoven with bluebells poppies and daffodils. Little bumble bees buried themselves into the flower's cups and two hover-birds fluttered each side of her head sharing the nectar with the bees. Her eyes were startling. Similar to the makers but also silver. In each eye were tiny images of the world slowly turning.

'What troubles you Ruby, why are you crying'? Ruby was mesmerised. She retold the conversation she had had with Lily. 'I sent you Ruby, I heard your master's plea for help'. Ruby plucked up the courage to ask who the angelic looking lady was. 'Some call me Mother Earth, others Mother Nature Ruby'. Ruby sobbed again, 'so are you my Mother who I saw in my dreams '? 'I am everyone's Mother Ruby'. 'Even the makers and keepers'?' 'Yes my child. You haven't been given magical looks because you represent the children that will soon be inheriting our world. All of the newcomers will be children Ruby. We will feed and nurture them using nature's mystical ways and there will be no winters until they become adults. They will learn to love and cherish the wonderful world you have all made for them. They will giggle at your butterflies trying hard to fly straight'. Ruby blushed a little again, but strangely her blush, instead of being a reddish colour took on a slight golden tinge similar to the makers. Mother smiled. 'All over the earth the children will smile and give thanks for the beauty that surrounds them: the forests, the glorious landscapes, the flowers and birds, the insects that you have helped to create, they will also learn to share and live in harmony with all life that the makers have worked so hard to offer our earth.

When they grow into adults the winters shall return. 'Why will the winters return Mother?' 'Winters freshen up the earth Ruby. It also gives a chance for animals to go to sleep. They will live underground and keep warm, even your bumble bee will bury itself and go to sleep. It will do them good, they will wake up when the warm weather returns and feel refreshed and ready to go about their business again.

The adults will build shelters for their children to keep them warm using only nature's renewable resources' ugh, thought Ruby, 'I'm sorry Mother but I don't understand what nature's reglueable rehorses means. 'haha renewable resources, it means Ruby they will only build shelters from materials that nature has gifted them. Materials, that with the keepers help will re-grow even stronger and more plentiful, like the branches of trees, reeds and thatch made of straw, any materials that won't be lost forever from our world. The homes will provide warmth and shelter in the cold winters'. Ruby began to understand her purpose in life. 'But what will happen to me when my work with master is finished'? 'Don't you worry Ruby I'll find you lots of jobs to do. You will live with me and watch over the new-comers. The work you have done so far for your master has been truly inspiring. The children will gradually be gifted imagination and creativity but if any struggle with these gifts you will visit them while they sleep and gently whisper in their ears your own imaginative ideas which will help them on their way. You shall be called Ruby the creator. Ruby was so overjoyed that she leapt onto a large toadstool at the bottom of the tree and onto Mothers lap giving her a big kiss. Mother Nature beamed with delight. 'Now Ruby, you must be on your way, master insect maker will be waiting for you, Lily will guide you back, and Ruby, don't forget your stick insect'!

Peter Plant

www.ingramcontent.com/pod-product-compliance
Lightning Source LLC
Chambersburg PA
CBHW042327150426
43193CB00001B/11